Joy of Flower Arrangement

Hiroko Fujita

Joy of Flower Arrangement

CONTENTS

© 1997 Graph-sha Ltd. All rights reserved.
Translated by Lynda Shoup Ooka
Published by Graph-sha Ltd., Tokyo, Japan
First edition, First printing: September 1997

Overseas distributor:
Japan Publications Trading Co., Ltd.,
1-2-1 Sarugaku-cho, Chiyoda-ku, Tokyo, Japan
Distributed in the United States by
Kodansha America, Inc., through Oxford
University Press, 198 Madison Avenue,
New York, NY 10016
ISBN 0-87040-990-5
Printed in Japan

About the Author

Hiroko Fujita is a floral artist who loves flowers and nature. Born in Yokohama, she was introduced to Japanese Flower Arrangement at a young age and later to Western flower arrangement by American housewives living in Yokohama. After graduating from Musashino Art University she started work as a floral artist. In addition to teaching at a variety of locations, she has taught at international symposiums using flowers to exchange culture. She is the founder of Takao Flower Arrangement School and a lecturer at NHK Culture Center.

Basic Arrangement Style

Spray Shape Style

Fountain Style

L Shaped Style

Semi-Spherical Style

Fan Style

Horizontal Style

Triangular Style

This chapter introduces how to make the seven fundamental styles of arrangements, a colonial bouquet, a boutonniere and a corsage. The arrangements are simple for anyone to assemble from easy to obtain popular flowers. Knowing just a few shapes is sure to change the way one approaches arrangements. After grasping the basic styles, individuality or personal sense may be explored.

Semi-Spherical Style

This semi-spherical structured arrangement mimics the shape of a hydrangea flower. The view from the top is circular while that from the side is semi-circular. As it can be viewed from any angle it is appropriate for dining or living room tables. If the color scheme is unbalanced it fails to look round. Take care to arrange it smoothly so as to make an impression of one continuous line.

Bridal Pink Semi-Spherical Arrangement

The pink of the Natira (spray carnation) perfectly matches the Bridal Pink (roses). When the Natira and the Bridal Pink are not available, use spray carnation and roses having similar pink color. The stem of spray carnation divides into 3 to 4 flowers each, making it very useful to add volume. Using a variety of greens yields a fuller color making it more beautiful.

Rose
If possible, use Bridal Pink rose. As the name indicates, this rose is suitable for weddings because it has a refined, lovely, soft color. It is useful for a large variety of treatments such as arrangements, bouquets and corsages.

Spray Carnation
The end of this carnation fans into 3 or more flowers per stem. It is a very useful, long lasting material coming in a large variety of colors and easy to use in any sort of arrangement.

Baby's Breath
There is no flower more suitable for displaying softness and luxury. The countless, small, white flowers spread out everywhere are pretty and elegant.

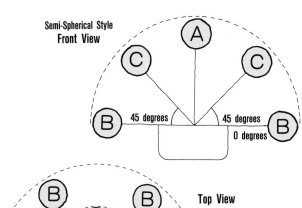

Semi-Spherical Style Front View

Asparagus Fern (above)
A green with innumerable, detailed leaves. Used for filling empty spaces in arrangements. Care in handling is required as there are thorns on the roots.

Eucalyptus (Top Left)
Leaves are round, grey-green. Used along with other greens it adds volume.

Leather Fern (Bottom Left)
Often used in arrangements and bouquets. The lower branches may be trimmed and used on their own, making this a very useful plant.

Top View

**F.P. (Focal Point) =
Focus of the Arrangement
(point C)**

Bridal Pink Semi-Spherical Arrangement

1

Floral Materials

11 Roses · 3~5 Spray Carnations · 1 Asparagus Fern · 1 Baby's Breath · 5 Leather Ferns · 2~3 small Eucalyptus

Set oasis in the vase so that it protrudes beyond the vase ¾~1″ (2~3 cm).

The minimum number of points needed to achieve a circle is 5 (3 yields a triangle and 4 a square). Cut a star shape into the oasis with a florist knife. The flowers will be inserted into this form to make the pentagon.

Container
White Compote Bowl

Arrangements are better and more beautiful when roses are 70~80% open. The Focal Point (FP) is the roses at a 45 degree angle. Carefully check flowers before arranging. Set aside the 5 most beautiful roses.

4

Top View

Front View

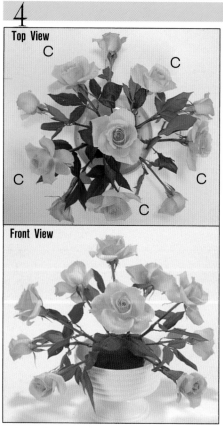

Take the 5 roses which you choose for the Focal Point and cut them in a similar manner using your palm to measure. Insert flowers between **A** and **B** at a 45 degree angle and between the **B**s in the circle (as indicated **C**).

5

Cut the spray carnations in a similar way and insert between each rose slightly further in.

6

Cut the asparagus fern shorter than the flowers and insert. Check that the asparagus fern does not reach out as far as the roses and for total balance.

2

Placing the central rose. Measure one hand's length from tip of the rose bud down stem, add 1～1½″(3～4cm) of stem to insert in oasis and cut. Remove extra leaves on the lower part of the stem. Insert in the center of the oasis at a right angle to the vase.
(See diagram p.5)

3

Top View

In the same manner, measure the 5 roses with your palm, cut and lay on the points of the star in the oasis. From the top view the flowers should form a circular pattern which can be connected by a line.

Front View

Insert the roses into the side of the oasis so that the stems just touch the vase and the flowers are horizontal.
(See diagram p.5)

7

Insert eucalyptus in the same fashion. This arrangement can be made without it, but a variety of greens adds to fullness.

8

Cut the 5 leather ferns a bit longer than the roses **B** and insert horizontally under the 5 roses.

9

Top View

Front View

Lastly, insert baby's breath all over in an elegant fashion, far enough back so it does not reach the flowers. Tidy up the shape so that it is truly semi-spherical to finish.

Spring Pink

Round Bouquet

Flowers gathered into circular shape are called a round bouquet. Flowers surrounded in the back by greens or net are called colonial bouquets. In addition, depending on the design they may be referred to by a variety of names such as tussy mussies or Victorian bouquets. The sweet, lovely round shape goes well with any dress.

Rose Colonial Bouquet

For a sweet, pink color roses and carnations were paired. This is a good choice for bridal outfits and color schemes. Recently, people can be seen carrying bouquets at parties. A pink bouquet is not so formal, so it is possible to make a casual fashion statement by carrying one.

From the left
Rose
Spray Carnation
Baby's Breath
Leather Fern
(Refer to page 5)

c o r s a g e 1

There is nothing so useful as a corsage for making formal events such as graduations, school entrance ceremonies, and recitals festive. And how much more luxurious when made with live flowers!

Rose Corsage

This corsage is to match the rose bouquet. As roses go with any dress they are an easy flower to work with, but carnations, fresia and seasonal flowers are among the variety of flowers which may be used to make this corsage.

Rose and Baby's Breath
(Refer to page 5)

Diamond Ivy
Also popular as an indoor houseplant. It keeps well and is an essential part of bouquets and corsages.

Smilax Asparagus
This soft, tender vine is an excellent choice for bridal bouquets.

See page 13 for instructions for Bridal Pink Corsage.

Rose Colonial Bouquet

Floral Materials / Other Materials

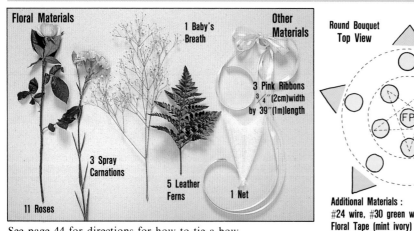

- 1 Baby's Breath
- Other Materials
- 3 Pink Ribbons ¾″(2cm)width by 39″(1m)length
- 3 Spray Carnations
- 5 Leather Ferns
- 1 Net
- 11 Roses

See page 44 for directions for how to tie a bow.

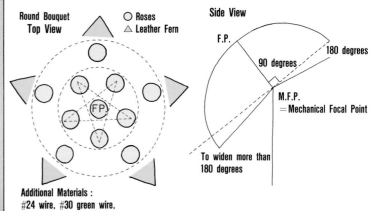

Round Bouquet Top View

○ Roses △ Leather Fern

FP

Side View

F.P.
90 degrees
180 degrees
M.F.P. = Mechanical Focal Point
To widen more than 180 degrees

Additional Materials :
#24 wire, #30 green wire,
Floral Tape (mint ivory)

---

1 Wiring and Taping

Rose

1 Remove leaves and calyces and cut the stem ¾ ~ 1″(2~3cm) beneath the flower.

2 Pierce the base of the flower with a # 24 wire and pull through to the center.

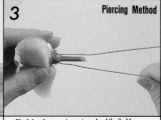

3 Piercing Method — Fold the wire in half following the stem's direction and wrap to enclose.(See page 30)

4 Starting at the base of the flower, wrap downward with floral tape.

Baby's Breath

1

2

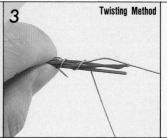

3 Twisting Method

1. Cut baby's breath to just palm size.
2. Fold a #24 wire in half and hook it into the stem.
3. Bend one half of the wire along the line of the stem. Use the other half of the wire to wrap around both. Starting from the top wrap the whole with floral tape.

Leather Fern

1

2

3 Twisting Method

1. Cut the fern to the length from fingertips to wrist and remove the bottom leaf.
2. Fold a #24 wire in half and hook it over the bottom branch.
3. Wrap the wire around the stem twice and stabilize with floral tape.

Wired Samples

- 11 Roses
- 17 Leather Ferns
- 8 Carnations wired in the same way as the roses
- 3 Baby's Breath

2 Putting it Together

Using 3 leather ferns, enclose one rose in a ring. Use 3 stalks of baby's breath to fill in the spaces and encircle the whole. The baby's breath should be distributed to protrude a bit past the rose.

The next 5 roses should be added somewhat further back than the middle rose. Balance the roses carefully in order to make a pentagon.

Enclose all with 6 sprigs of leather fern. Even at this stage this is a beautiful bouquet.

Use 8 carnations to carefully balance and enclose all. The flowers should become gradually lower as they approach the periphery.

Add the remaining 5 roses around the periphery. Make the top view circular and the overall shape a beautiful semi-circle.

Use the remaining leather fern to surround the outer edge. The ends of the fern should protrude a bit.

3 Wrapping with Tape

Adjust the flowers all around and bind the stems with a #30 wire.

Cut the stems evenly about 1″ (3cm) beneath a one hand grasp.

Bind with floral tape starting at the top of the stems and working down.

At the bottom, turn and wrap back upwards to finish at the base.

4 Wrapping the ribbon around the handle

1

2

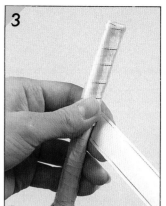

3

4

Cut 39″(1m) of ribbon. Place the end of the bouquet at the 1¼″ (3cm) mark and fold back wrapping up the stem.

Gripping the folded end, adjust the edge and start wrapping the ribbon from this point.

Turning the bouquet around, wrap carefully all the way up to the end tightly enough so that it does not unfasten.

With one hand, firmly grip the wrapped end and with the other, pull the end of the ribbon through the last loop.

5

6

Pull the ribbon to secure. Make sure to pull tightly enough to completely fasten it.

Cut the leftover ribbon.

5 Attaching the Net

Open the net and insert the handle in the opening.

6 Attaching the Ribbon

(Ribbon tying instructions p.44)

Prepare a ribbon in the manner shown on page 44. Ensure that the ribbon will not slide or fall, attach below the top of the handle's ribbon. Cut the loop in the middle.

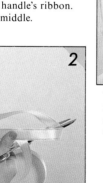

To make for easy holding, bend the bouquet above the ribbon at a 60 degree angle.

Rose Corsage

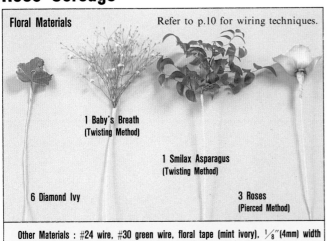

Floral Materials

Refer to p.10 for wiring techniques.

1 Baby's Breath
(Twisting Method)

1 Smilax Asparagus
(Twisting Method)

6 Diamond Ivy

3 Roses
(Pierced Method)

Other Materials : #24 wire, #30 green wire, floral tape (mint ivory), 1/8″(4mm) width silver ribbon 47″(1.2m) and 27 1/2″(70cm)

Corsages are made to the size of one's own palm. It is easy to make them a suitable shape and size this way. Using live flowers, it is important to carefully do the wring and taping.

1

Fold a #24 wire in half, pierce through the center of the ivy leaf and pull through.

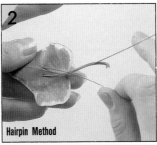

2

Hairpin Method

Cross the wires in the back. Run one wire along the stem and wrap them with the other. Wrap the whole with floral tape.

3

Wire 3 or 4 ivy leaves in the manner described above. Make the size and shape in proportion to the palm of your hand.

4

Wire one piece of smilax in the manner described for leather fern on page 10 and add to ivy in keeping with proportion.

5

Do the same with baby's breath. Grasp firmly at the base of the greens while making the additions.

6

Place rosebud on top. As always, judge size and shape refering to the size of your palm.

7

Add two roses a bit lower and at an angle.

8

Add 3 ivy leaves in front of the roses. Adjust each individually to lean forward.

9

Now all the live materials are assembled. Check the overall balance and tidy up the shape.

10

Secure by twisting a #30 wire at the base, cut the excess wire and wrap with tape.

11

To achieve a full front view when worn, hold the corsage by the stems and bend the flowers to an appropriate angle.

12

Fan the wire out pleasingly and cut on an angle 2 1/4 ～ 2 3/4″(6 ～7cm) below the flowers.

13

Attach a ribbon made as directed on page 44. Place a corsage pin on the back.

14

Adjust the shape. When pinning to clothing the stem faces upward and the flowers down.

Horizontal Style

Rose

If possible, use the Sonia rose. The fresh salmon pink color of this rose adds brilliant elegance to any sort of party. It even retains its beautiful color when dried.

African Daisy (pink color)

This large-faced flower can be inserted for accent at key points. It comes in rich colors.

Miniature Chrysanthemums

These small, white circles are cute flowers. They are sweet in arrangements, bouquets or corsages.

Ladder Fern

This green has a long, thin, neat shape. Keeping one as a houseplant can come in handy.

This horizontal spreading arrangement is suitable for use on the table. The middle is tall and flattens out as it expands to each side. When seen from above it is oval shaped. Considering that a table arrangement is meant to add to the enjoyment of meals, flowers with strong colors and scents should be avoided. In order to be able to see the person across the table when seated, the arrangement should be no higher than chest level.

Horizontal Arrangement using Roses

Using roses and matching shade african daisy a salmon pink color scheme was achieved. When using flowers of a variety of colors, arrange them so as they compliment each other and enhance each other's beauty. Greens should be inserted so as not to protrude as far as the flowers. You can enjoy a gorgeous, volumunous arrangement.

**Horizontal Style
Front View**

45 degrees 45 degrees

20 degrees 0-15 degrees

Top View

○ Rose
△ African Daisy
△ F.P. = African Daisy

If a low vase is used, the flowers can be arranged so low as to lay on or nearly touch the table.

Asparagus
A plant with detailed, dense leaves. Very useful for adding volume to arrangements.

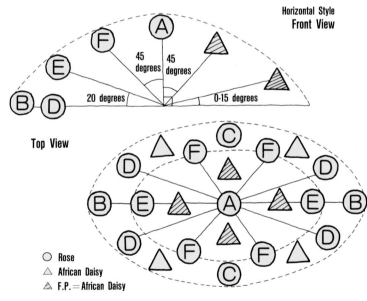

Elegant Pink

Horizontal Arrangement using Roses

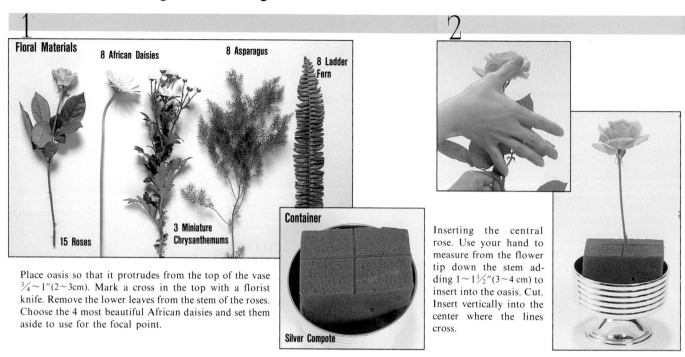

1 Floral Materials

8 African Daisies

8 Asparagus

8 Ladder Fern

15 Roses

3 Miniature Chrysanthemums

Container

Silver Compote

Place oasis so that it protrudes from the top of the vase ¾~1″(2~3cm). Mark a cross in the top with a florist knife. Remove the lower leaves from the stem of the roses. Choose the 4 most beautiful African daisies and set them aside to use for the focal point.

2

Inserting the central rose. Use your hand to measure from the flower tip down the stem adding 1~1½″(3~4 cm) to insert into the oasis. Cut. Insert vertically into the center where the lines cross.

6

Top View

View from an Angle

Front View

E   E

For **E** cut 2 roses 1 flower length shorter than **D** and insert between **A** and **B** slanting it at a 20 degree angle from **B**.

7

Outer ring of African daisies

Inserting the 4 African daisies. Insert one at a time close to **F** so as to maintain the oval shape at a 15 degree angle sloped.

8

Inner ring of African daisies

The 4 African daisies used for the focal point are half the length of flowers **AB** and **AC** and inserted at a 45 degree angle. This completes the basic line.

3

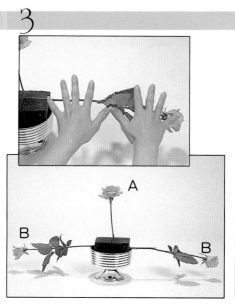

Cut roses into 2 hand's lengths. Insert horizontally on both sides resting on the rim of the vase.

4

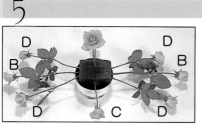

Cut rose into 1 hand's length. Insert at a right angle from **B** on both sides into the cross mark.

5

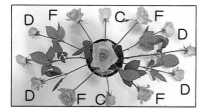

Cut 4 roses one flower length shorter than **B** and insert on either side (**D**) of each **B**.

For **F**, cut 4 roses 2 flower lengths shorter than **D**. Insert them at a 45 degree angle to the vase between **C** and **D**. The view from above should be a beautiful oval.

9

Separate the miniature chrysanthemums into small branches and fill in the holes. Insert them so as to keep the oval shape when viewed from both top and side.

10

Separate asparagus into small branches and fill in as with miniature chrysanthemums. Take care to balance flowers and greens as you go.

11

Top View

View from an Angle

Front View

Insert the ladder fern under the roses **BCD** so that it comes out just a bit further than the roses. Adjust overall shape.

17

Spray Shape Style

Sunshine of Yellow

This is a basket arrangement. Although the flowers and stems are inserted separately, the point is to make them appear as one continuous line. It is made to be viewed from a diagonal side. The view from the top is shown to be triangular in the photo on the left, but depending on the floral materials its shape may vary. Please arrange the stems and flowers according to their form. Whether set in a bay window, on a shelf or on the floor, it is sure to create atmosphere.

Sunflower Spray Shape

Summer sunflowers have recently been seen in flower shops nearly year round. Use the clean lines of this flower in this arrangement.
Yellow ball are like yellow pompons. Pollen drops easily from these flowers, so be careful about where this arrangement is displayed. This is also attractive using roses or calla lilies.

Sunflower
Reflective of its name, its color and size are like the sun. It is very effective for use in arrangements for large event spaces and displays. As it is a flower with a strong presence, take care to choose flowers which will not clash.

Yellow Ball
Yellow globes on the end of the stem make these flowers interesting. These will do the trick when something different is desired for an arrangement.

Gold-dust Dracaena
An oval leaf with yellow spots. It is shiny and long lasting. Cut into branches of 2 or 3 to use in the arrangement.

Window Plant
A large leaf with a unique shape. Use this distinctive leaf to advantage. Depending on the arrangement style, this leaf can be very interesting.

Spray Shape Style
Side View

○ Sunflower

F.P.

45 degrees 90 degrees

0 degrees

Top View

F.P.

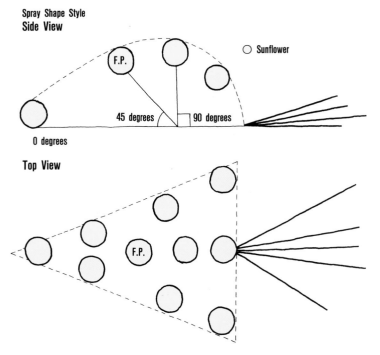

Sunflower Spray Shape

1

Floral Materials

10 Sunflowers

5 Gold-dust Dracaena

8 Yellow Ball

1 Window Plant

Fold cellophane in two and place under oasis. This contains leaks and is attractive.

Container
Basket

3

Measure a sunflower to one hand's length adding 1~1½″(3~4cm) to insert in the oasis and cut. Insert in the center of the top side of the oasis with the flower facing forward.

4

As in **3**, cut flowers one hand's length. Insert on either side of the central sunflower one at a time in a horizontal fashion.

8

Insert 1 window plant under the **2** sunflower. It should protrude slightly in front of the sunflower.

9

Separate the gold-dust dracaena and insert randomly between the flowers. Insert them so as not to protrude farther than the flowers.

10

Insert yellow balls randomly so as not to extend past the sunflowers and beautifully balanced on left and right.

2

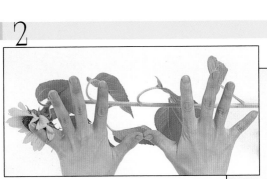

Measure a sunflower two hands' length adding 1~1½″(3~4cm) extra to insert in the oasis and cut. Insert flower horizontally into the side of the oasis in the middle so that the flower faces upwards.

The difference between oasis and needlepoint holders is that all sides of the oasis can be used. By inserting flowers into the side they can be arranged horizontally or even sloping lower.

5

Insert the 5th and 6th flowers between **3** and **4** so as to form an isosceles triangle.

6

Cut sunflower to ⅔ the length of **2** and insert the flower for the focal point at a 45 degree angle. Insert a flower slightly back on either side.

7

Insert one flower at an angle in back of the handle. This completes the 10 flower outline.

11

Insert sunflower stalks from behind. Cut stalks to be balanced when seen from the front and arrange at an angle which makes them look attached to flowers in the front. To create a natural look, cut them at various lengths, long and short.

12

Adjust overall from front view to finish.

Bright Yellow

This arrangement is shaped like the letter "L". As it is meant to be seen straight on, it is placed in entryways or places in which there is a wall behind it. To enhance the beautiful line, use long, straight materials. An example of reversed L shape can be seen on page 57. In either case, the focal point is at the intersection.

Gladiolus and Candlestick Lily L Shape

Similar colors were chosen for this arrangement. The room becomes sunny in a flash. The thin, long straight leaves of the gladiolus are used as a green, so few floral materials are needed. If alstroemeria is not available, it can be done well using lilies alone. Enjoy using flowers which have a beautiful line, such as delphinium or liatris in place of gladiolus.

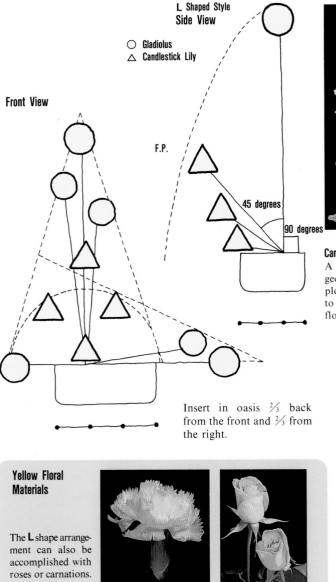

**L Shaped Style
Side View**

○ Gladiolus
△ Candlestick Lily

Front View

F.P.

45 degrees

90 degrees

Insert in oasis ⅔ back from the front and ⅔ from the right.

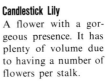

Gladiolus
A tall floral material good for large arrangements. Single flowers may also be used to advantage in bouquets and corsages.

Candlestick Lily
A flower with a gorgeous presence. It has plenty of volume due to having a number of flowers per stalk.

Alstroemeria
This recently popular flower comes in a wide range of varieties and colors. Each stem has multiple buds making it useful for building volume.

Yellow Floral Materials

The L shape arrangement can also be accomplished with roses or carnations.

Carnation

Rose

Gladiolus and Candlestick Lily **L** Shape

1

Floral Materials

6 Gladiolus

Some Gladiolus leaves

4 Candlestick Lilies

2 Alstroemeria

Using a florist knife, make a line in the oasis ⅔ from the front and ⅔ from the right.

Container
White Compote

Set the oasis so as to come 1 ~ 1½″(3 ~ 4 cm) above the top of the container.

2

Break off the buds on the tip of the gladiolus. Separate gladiolus leaves and set all aside.

4

Insert in the ⅔ line.

Cut a gladiolus slightly longer than ⅔ of **3** and insert horizontally in the right side of the oasis so as to just touch the container.

5

Cut a gladiolus less than ½ the length of **4** and insert horizontally in the left side. Insert so as to be in line with the ⅔ line and just touch the edge of the container.

7

Insert a gladiolus leaf in back of each flower so as to extend slightly beyond the flower. When seen from the side the arrangement should appear a single line.

8

Insert 1 lily on the right at a 45 degree angle of such a length so as not to disturb the **L** shape.

3

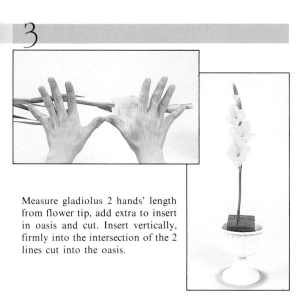

Measure gladiolus 2 hands' length from flower tip, add extra to insert in oasis and cut. Insert vertically, firmly into the intersection of the 2 lines cut into the oasis.

An arrangement using only gladiolus and candlestick lilies. By using a gladiolus with a hint of orange the arrangement became gorgeous.

6

Cut one gladiolus the same length as **4** and insert along **3** on the left. At the same time, cut another ⅔rds the length of **4** and insert along **4** on the right.

9

Cut the second lily to one hand's length and insert in front at a 45 degree angle. This becomes the focal point.

10

Cut another lily slightly shorter than **9** and insert between **9** and the gladiolus at a 30 degree angle.

11

Cut one lily leaving just enough stem to insert into oasis and insert in the front horizontally under **9**.

12

Add alstroemeria to the lower right side, touch up the overall shape.

Fountain Style

Soft Violet

Arranged using the image of a fountain, spreading out from the center to the four directions. The middle is high, dropping down as it widens out to the circumference. This arrangement can be viewed from all 360 degrees, but the front and back are the view points. When arranging in the basket, wrap in aluminum foil, place cellophane down or use oasis to avoid water leakage. Try a variety of solutions which suit the application.

Cosmos Fountain Style

Living in the city it is hard to come in contact with the 7 wild grasses of autumn. Using flowers from the garden and roadside creates a cheerful arrangement. This arrangement uses the image of the autumn flower cosmos. If some of the floral materials are unavailable, pick wild grass from a field.

Cosmos
Cosmos swaying in the breeze is very popular with women as a symbol of autumn. Used in presents or natural arrangements.

Gentian
An autumn flower suitable for either Japanese or Western arrangements. The deep blue purple ties it all together.

Abutilon
A violet, elegant flower. It damages with handling, so treat it with care.

Aster
Usable in large or small, Japanese or Western arrangements, it is a very useful flower. It projects brilliance.

Misty Blue
This flower is like a light purple veil. It yields a soft, quiet feeling to arrangements.

**Fountain Style
Side View**

Front View

Bupleurum
In color and size it is a toned down flower. It lasts a long time so try using it as an accent.

F.P.

45 degrees

0 degrees

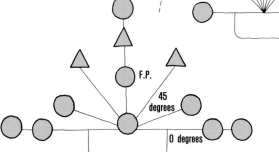

○ Aster
△ Gentian
○ Cosmos

Cosmos Fountain Style

1

Floral Materials

10~15
Abutilon

1 Misty Blue

15~25
Cosmos

2 Aster

2 Gentian

2~3
Bupleurum

As the basket is deep, add aluminum foil balls to raise the bottom taking care to create a flat surface. When additional height is desired, make balls of newspaper and wrap with aluminum foil. Lay an oasis base in the basket so as to be slightly lower than the edge of the basket. Cut oasis to protrude ¾~1″(2~3 cm) above the base and set it in.

Container
Round Basket

4

Cut the gentian to ⅔rds the length of the aster, and the remainder in half.

5

Put the ⅔rds length gentian in front of the aster.

Set it at a 45~60 degree angle.

6

Insert the remaining 2 gentians on either side of **5** at the same angle stretching out to the sides.

9

Inserting the focal point cosmos.

Cut the most beautiful cosmos one hand's length and insert in front of the gentian. When seen from the side the cosmos and gentian should form a gentle curve.

10

Insert cosmos so as to barely touch the edge of the basket.

Cut 2 cosmos to the same length as **8** and insert on the left and right sides horizontally behind the handle.

2

Estimate the size of the arrangement with the hands. The height will be 2 hands' length from the basket rim, and from the center point 2 hands' length to both the right and the left.

3

Insert from in back of the handle.

Measure flowers upside down. Cut aster two hands' length plus insertion length and insert vertically in the middle.

7

Cut the other gentian in the same fashion and arrange in the same way on the other side of the basket.

View from the side. Make the angle of all gentians symmetrical.

8

Adding cosmos. Cut 1⅔ hand's length and insert between the asters and the gentians.

11

Cut cosmos one hand's length and insert it horizontally under **9**.

Cut 2 cosmos the same length and insert horizontally in the front on the right and left.

12

Do the same in the back. In addition to the 2 cosmos on the full side, add 5 more.

Fullness from Front View

(Continued on next page)

13

Fill spaces with cosmos and abutilon. Fill to overflowing.

Add misty blue for softness. Add bupleurum to fill in the empty space.

14

Side View

Fill the back in the same fashion. This is also a wonderful arrangement when using field flowers. Touch up the overall shape to finish.
To create a smaller arrangement, all can be cut to shorter lengths.

Front View

Dendrobium Phalaenopsis Corsage

By making a corsage using the size of one's palm, the size and shape can be well accomplished. Pinning the corsage with the stem close to the collarbone and with the flower hanging down, accentuates the face. Dendrobium phalaenopsis can be worn to any kind of event, making it very versatile. White dendrobium phalaenopsis looks nice with colorful clothing. The ribbon can be gold or silver to match accessories or taste.

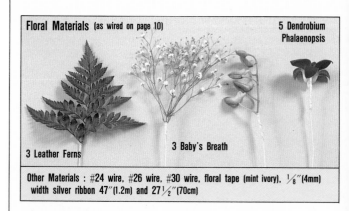

Floral Materials (as wired on page 10)

5 Dendrobium Phalaenopsis

3 Leather Ferns

3 Baby's Breath

Other Materials : #24 wire, #26 wire, #30 wire, floral tape (mint ivory), 1/8″(4mm) width silver ribbon 47″(1.2m) and 27 1/2″(70cm)

Wiring

1

Hairpin Method

Leaving 4~5 buds of dendrobium phalaenopsis on the end of the stalk, pluck off the remaining flowers one by one. Fold a #26 wire in half and insert through the center of the flower.

2

Piercing the flower, pull the wire all the way through.

3

Hold one wire along the stem and wrap together with remaining wire. Prepare buds, leather fern, and baby's breath with a #24 wire as on page 10.

1

Place a leather fern, wired as on page 10, on the palm.

2

Pile 1 baby's breath, the bud and 2 flowers of dendrobium phalaenopsis on top of the leather fern.

3

Add 1 baby's breath on top. Shape echoing the shape of the hand.

4

Add 2 more dendrobium on the whole. Position them somewhat lower making all more in keeping with the shape of the hand.

5

Add 2 leather ferns at the base. Adjust the overall shape so it looks beautiful.

6

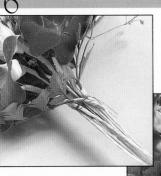

Secure the stalks with a # 30 wire wrapping tightly. Cut excess wire.

Wrap wire with floral tape. Bend wire and angle the flowers. Cut extra wire at $2\frac{1}{2} \sim 2\frac{3}{4}''$ ($6 \sim 7$cm).

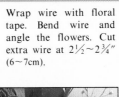

7

Attach ribbon and fix overall shape.

See page 44 for ribbon tying.

This arrangement is fan shaped, so it is also refered to as radiating style or peacock style. To be viewed from the front, it is a full direction, gorgeous looking design which works well for party halls, exhibition halls and public spaces. At home it suits entryways, guest rooms and living room shelves. For making small arrangements, choose thin-stemmed cute flowers.

Stock Fan Style

All white flowers were chosen for this arrangement. Even so, the white of the stock, the rose, the carnation and the baby's breath are all subtly different. Using a variety of floral materials depth of color develops. The phoenix in the back ties it all together. It is an elegant and gorgeous arrangement. Try using snapdragon or delphinium as a variaton.

Stock
A flower with clean, stretching elegance. There is an abundance of varieties and colors. Making the most of its straight line makes it good for arrangements or concerts. It does not absorb water well, so some extra care is neccesary.

Carnation
Use single white carnations. They are easy to blend with any flower or green. When arranging high in an arrangement choose flowers with sturdy stems.

Rose (Tineke)
There is nothing more elegant and chic than a white rose. A given for bridal parties, roses bring nobility and refinement to any arrangement.

Phoenix Roebelenii
A leaf with movement, it brings activity to an arrangement. The ends of the leaf were unkempt, so they were cut evenly.

Baby's Breath see page 5.

Fan Style

Snow White

Stock Fan Style

1

Floral Materials

18 Stock | 2 Baby's Breath | 6 Roses | 5 Carnations | 5 Phoenix Roebelenii

The oasis stands ¾~1″(2~3cm) above the vase. Cut a line into the oasis ⅔ from the front. The main flowers are inserted along this line. Place oasis in vase and fix in place using additional oasis and tape.

Vase
Soup Tureen

5

Side View

Cut **A2** about 1″(3cm) shorter than **A** and insert in front of **A** at a 10 degree angle leaning to the front. Cut **A3** about 1″(3cm) shorter than **A2** and insert leaning forward at a 45 degree angle. Cut the stem of **A4** just long enough for inserting into the oasis and insert horizontally in the front so that only the flower is showing.

6

Cut 4 the same length as **A2**. Insert 2 at the same angle on either side of the stock in the back (**C2**, **D2**).

9

Insert 1 rose between **A2** and **A3**, and 1 carnation between **A3** and **A4** so as not to exceed the line made by the stock when viewed from the side.

10

Insert 1 rose between **A3** and the carnation. Add the 4 roses symmetrically on either side for a sense of serene balance.

11

Insert the 4 carnations symmetrically on either side. Roses and carnations can be inserted around the focal point in a somewhat free style.

2

Measure 2 hands' length from the tip and cut.

Insert vertically in the middle of the line marked in the oasis.

A

3

A

B   B

Cut 2 stocks to 2 hands' lengths and insert horizontally in the side of the oasis on both left and right **B**.

4

C   A   C

D   D

B   B

Cut 4 more the same length, insert between **A** and **B** dividing the space in 3rds. **C** will be a 60 degree angle and **D** a 30 degree angle creating a fan shape. Insert 2 at a time.

7

Cut 2 the same length as **A3**, insert at a consistant 45 degree angle on either side of **A3** and between **C2** and **D2** (**C3**). At the same time, add 2 cut to the same length as **A3**, horizontally one on either side(**D3**). These 18 stock flowers have completed the outline.

8

Cut the baby's breath into smaller sections and fill in the spaces over the whole so as not to exceed the line created by the stock.

12

Insert 5 phoenix roebelenii in the back. Cut them a bit longer than the stock. When viewed from the side the phoenix roebelenii makes a straight line. Check for good balance from the front view. Adjust shape accordingly to finish.

Dendrobium Phalaenopsis Bridal Bouquet

The bridal bouquet is a key point in the appearance of a bride. Take the body type, dress and image of the bride into careful consideration to make a heartfelt bouquet. Make it lovely, crisp and elegant. Choose long lasting flowers, mist after constructing and store in a cool spot if possible. If a bouquet stand is not available, use something such as a wine bottle to hold it so it won't loose its shape.

1

11 Dendrobium Phalaenopsis
(Hairpin Method)

4 Smilax Asparagus
(Twisting Method)

13 Leather Ferns
(Twisting Method)

Wire the number of flowers and greens stated above referring to pages 10 and 30 for directions.

2

Surround the central dendrobium phalaenopsis with 4 smilax asparagus positioned somewhat lower than the flower.

3

Arrange 5 dendrobium phalaenopsis in a pentagon shape and encircle with 8 leather ferns.

4

Surround with 5 more dendrobium phalaenopsis spacing them in between and slightly lower than **3**.

6

Secure at the base by wrapping with wire. Cut to an even length and wrap with floral tape.

7

As shown on page 12, wrap ribbon around the stems cleanly enclosing the end.

8

At the end, bring the ribbon through the loop and pull secure. Cut excess ribbon.

9

Insert handle through net. Tie a ribbon at base (see page 44). Secure ribbon so as not to slip off.

Boutonniere

For the boutonniere the groom wears on his jacket lapel, a single flower from the bride's bouquet is arranged as compactly as possible. Depending on the clothing, a single flower or greens alone can be very attractive.

Floral Materials (Prewired)

1 Dendrobium Phalaenopsis
1 Smilax Asparagus
1 Leather Fern
1/2" (1cm) wide nonslip ribbon, white, 24" (60cm)

1

Arrange the leather fern, smilax asparagus and dendrobium phalaenopsis in that order and secure with a #30 wire.

2

Cut wires even 2~2¼" (5~6cm) below the flower. Wrap the stems with white floral tape.

3

As it will not be wrapped with ribbon, the tape should be wrapped carefully.

Snow White

5

Place 5 leather ferns under the 5 dendrobium inserted in **4**. When seen from the side it looks like the diagram on page 10.

10

Holding the handle, bend to a 60 degree angle. Check overall shape to finish.

4

Wrap a ribbon at the base and tie in a butterfly bow. Attach boutonniere pin, if neccessary.

Diagrams, see page 10.

Warmth
of Red

Triangular Style

This is a triangular design. The wide variety of possibilities makes this and interesting design as equilateral triangles, isoscles triangles or scalene triangles can be chosen to emphasize the sharpness, softness or cuteness of the floral materials. Meant to be viewed from the front, place where the back faces a wall. Looks lovely displayed in entryways or bay windows.

Christmas Triangular Arrangement

This arrangement uses fir and a deep red rose appropriate for Christmas, Holly dyed silver are used for interest. Red alchemilla berries have been used, but other berries or artificial flowers may be used. Use this arrangement in place of a Christmas tree for creating a festive mood.

Rose
An elegant, fulled budded red rose. Attractive in corsages, bouquets and any sort of arrangement.

Alchemilla (berries)
Nothing is as useful as alchemilla berries for Christmas, New Year's or Winter arrangements. Take care in handling, as the berries drop off easily. The leaves can also be used as greens.

Holly
Essential ingredient for Christmas arrangements. As the ends of the leaves are sharply pointed, extra care must be taken when using in a corsage.

Fir
Essential ingredient for Christmas tree, wreaths and decorations. As a long lasting plant, if handled with care it can be reused the next season.

▲ Asparagus Fern (p.5)

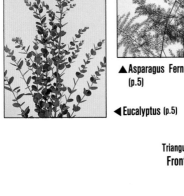

◀ Eucalyptus (p.5)

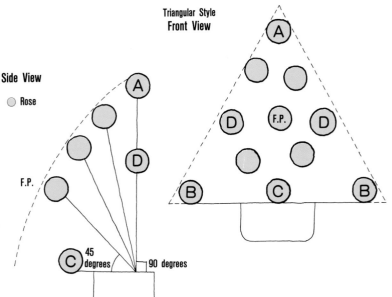

Side View

⬤ Rose

Triangular Style
Front View

Deep Red Floral Materials

In addition to roses, flowers such as carnations, African daisies and tulips may be used in triangular arrangement.

Tulip

Carnation

African Daisy

Christmas Triangular Arrangement

1

Floral Materials

2 small stalks Eucalyptus

1 branch Fir

11 Roses

6 Stalks Alchemilla Berries

3 small stalks Holly

Additional Floral Materials : 3 stalks Asparagus Fern

Place the oasis in the vase so as to protrude 1~1½″(3~4cm) from the top. Fill extra space with additional oasis to secure. Using a florist knife, cut a line in the oasis ⅔rds to the back.

Container
Soup Tureen

4

Holding a rose upside down, measure and cut to the size of **3**. Place in front leaning to the left of the first rose. Insert so as to be a flower head shorter than **3**.

5

In the same fashion cut a rose measuring to **4** and insert on the right. Insert in front of **4** and angle to the right.

6

Measure the most beautiful rose in the same way to the length of **5** and insert at a 45 degree angle. It is the focal point.

9

To form a triangle shape with the line of the flowers, cut 2 roses to appropriate lengths and insert between **3** and **8**.

10

Cut 2 roses to the same length as **9**.

Insert one, on each side of **6** symmetrically at a 45~50 degree angle. They should be a flower head's length shorter than **9**.

When seen from the side, the flowers form a gentle curve with the bottom flower being pulled in.

2

Dying the holly silver. Spread a newspaper and spray paint holly thoroughly. Leave to dry.

3

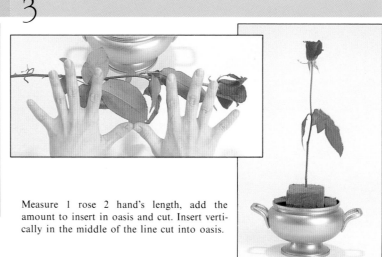

Measure 1 rose 2 hand's length, add the amount to insert in oasis and cut. Insert vertically in the middle of the line cut into oasis.

7

Cut 1 rose a bit shorter than **6** and insert horizontally in the side of the oasis in the front.

Seen from the side the bottom rose looks drawn into the arrangement.

8

Cut 2 roses to a hand's length plus extra for inserting into oasis. Insert one on each side vertically into the line cut into the oasis.

11

Cut the asparagus fern to suitable lengths and insert between the flowers so as not to protrude past the line of the triangle.

12

Insert 1 eucalyptus on each side. As the basic triangle is formed by the roses, insert so as not to break the form.

13

Add alchemilla berries. Place 6 stems of alchemilla for effect being careful of overall balance.

(Continued on next page)

14

Stand a large fir centered in the back to protrude slightly farther than **8**. Insert 1 branch horizontally on each side.

15

Back View

Add 3 silver sprayed holly branches for accent. Adjust overall shape.

Check that the greens do not protrude past the flowers from the side view.

Side View

Completed

Christmas Corsage

This is a red and green corsage arranged for Christmas. Christmas parties are popular. Appropriate for small children and adults this corsage is very handy. For children make it small and attach a safety pin. Wrapped prettily it is sure to please.

The carnation is feathered. Feathering is dividing a flower and reconstructing into 2 or 3 flowers. It is useful for bouquets, corsages and small arrangements.

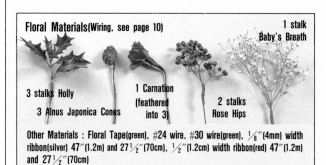

Floral Materials(Wiring, see page 10)

3 stalks Holly

3 Alnus Japonica Cones

1 Carnation (feathered into 3)

2 stalks Rose Hips

1 stalk Baby's Breath

Other Materials : Floral Tape(green), #24 wire, #30 wire(green), 1/8″(4mm) width ribbon(silver) 47″(1.2m) and 27 1/2″(70cm), 1/2″(1.2cm) width ribbon(red) 47″(1.2m) and 27 1/2″(70cm)

1

Arrange 3 holly leaves on the palm of your hand raised in the center.

2

Add the 3 alnus japonica cones and 3 carnations for good balance.

5

Secure all at base with wire and cover with floral tape. Separate stems and cut at a length of 2~2 1/4 (5~6cm). Add corsage pin at this spot.

When wiring alnus japonica cones refer to page 66. Hook the wire around the cone.

Carnation Feathering

1

Separate a carnation into 3 sections.

2

Wrap the roots of one section with a #28 wire 2~3 times.

3

Twist wire 2~3 times at bese and match wires together.

4

Using another #28 wire, pierce the flower at the base of the petals.

5

Fold wire in half and run along the first wire.

6

Take one half of the second wire to wrap the other 3 wires together.

7

Wrap from top downwards with green floral tape.

8

Finish to desired length. Finish the others to make 3 flowers.

3

Wire rose hips branch and wrap with floral tape. Add rose hips.

4

Add baby's breath all over to cover and protrude past flowers to add softness.

6

With the 2 ribbons form a bow as on page 44. Tie at base. Adjust shape to finish.

Ribbon Tying

This is ribbon for tying on the handle of bouquets. As it can also be used for simple bouquets and wrapping presents it is useful to remember.

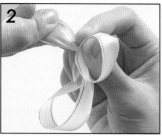

1

Holding the end of the ribbon, form a small loop. Flip over once to make the outside of the ribbon face outwards.

2

Make a slightly large loop under the first loop. Hold with the middle finger and flip the ribbon over once.

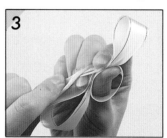

3

Making sure that the outside of the ribbon is showing, make another loop of the same size on the other side.

4

In the same fashion, make 2 more loops on each side growing gradually larger. Holding firmly with the middle finger, make a large circle form the next section of ribbon.

5

While still holding firmly, cut the remaining ribbon $\frac{3}{4}$~1"(2~3cm) from the middle. This end will be hidden so leave so leave it as is.

6

Holding in the middle, pull an ornamental ribbon through the smallest loop.

7

Pull ribbon through to desired length and cut. There are still no ties in this ribbon, so do not let off pressure, but keep holding firmly.

8

Tie the central loop with the loose ribbon. Carefully use the hand holding the ribbon when tying.

9

Tie tightly once more to finish.

10

When using, cut the last circle. Make according to use and in a variety of arrangements.

Arrangement Applications

After mastering fundamental styles, make arrangements which fit your needs and fully express your own sense. As room accents, presents, and when entertaining, there are many chances for flowers to be the right touch. Adding more flowers to our lifestyle brings a sense of nature, the changing seasons and adds charm to every day.

How to Choose Flowers

Flower arrangement begins with the choice of flowers. Choose taking into consideration the color and design of the arrangement, the place it will be displayed, the length of display and the season. As with choosing vegetables, the most important consideration is freshness. As they are living things, try to buy the freshest ones come directly from the market.

Flower
Beautiful color, buds open 70% are desirable.

Calyx
Closed and firm is best.

Pompon Type Flower
Choose buds which are 70-80% open. Not all buds may be in blossom at the same time.

Spray Carnation

Stem
Depending on the variety, but straight is preferred. When held from the bottom, it should stand straight on its own.

Larkspur

Alexandrian Laurel

It is important to find a good flower shop. Locate one which matches your taste and consult with their staff. If you explain in detail what you are looking for you can receive valuable advice.

Leaf
Choose a vividly colored and strong leaf.

Oasis

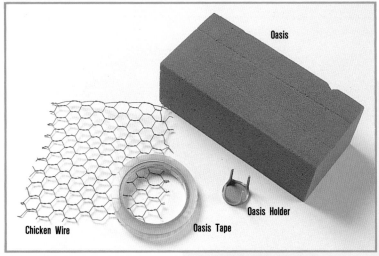

Oasis

Oasis Holder

Oasis Tape

Chicken Wire

Oasis is the tool with which to secure flowers in flower arrangement. One piece is about the size of box of tissues. Being made of synthetic resin, it is very light. One of its notable features is that not only the top, but all sides can be used for inserting flowers. Its ability to absorb water makes it possible to achieve a wide range of arrangements. However, care must be taken, as once it has been pierced a hole remains which cannot be fixed. Oasis is secured by oasis tape or an oasis holder according to the container.

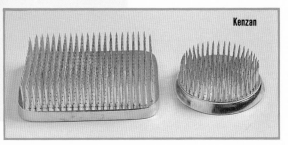

Kenzan

Chicken Wire Chicken Wire is used to wrap around oasis or made into a ball, inserted into a vase and used to secure flowers. Choose method according to function.

Kenzan (Needlepoint Holder) Used in Japanese Flower Arrangement (Ikebana) from long ago, kenzan come in a variety of shapes and sizes. It can be used immediately and lasts for some years.

①

②

Using Oasis

① Using a sharp blade, cut oasis to the size of the vase. A height of 1″(3cm) higher than the edge of the vase makes it easy to use.
② Soak in plenty of water for at least 30 minutes so as to penetrate to the core. To be certain of good results add a weight.

Oasis Base

This is a container with prongs to secure oasis. Inexpensive and light it is handy for arrangements which are given as presents or arranged in baskets, as shown. Any of the basic styles can be made using an oasis base.

Oasis Tape

This tape does not come off even when wet. It is useful to secure oasis when using a wide mouthed vase or making a large arrangement.

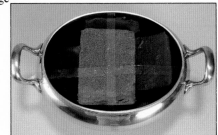

Florist Knife and Scissors

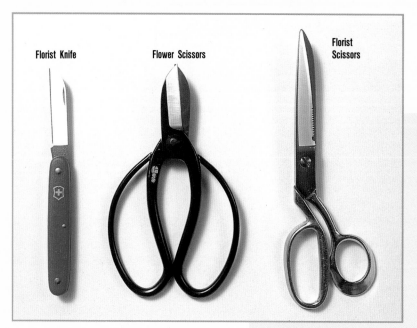

Florist Knife   **Flower Scissors**   **Florist Scissors**

The cut of the stem is an essential point. Cutting on a sharp angle allows for a larger surface for water absorption and is easier to insert in oasis. It is important to make a clean cut so as not to bruise the veins of the stem.

Florist Knife Used to cut flower, stem and branch. With just this one tool, most floral materials can be managed.

Flower Scissors Used for Japanese Flower Arrangement(Ikebana). Used when cutting materials such as thick branches.

Florist Scissors The blade has a zigzagged edge in the rear which can be used to cut wire. The tips can be used to cut ribbons or tulle. Very useful for flower designing.

Whether scissors or knife, maintaining a sharp edge is essential. After each use remove dampness and be sure not to neglect proper care.

Rose Stripper

Handling flowers which have thorny branches can be painful. This item can be useful to those who are troubled by thorns.

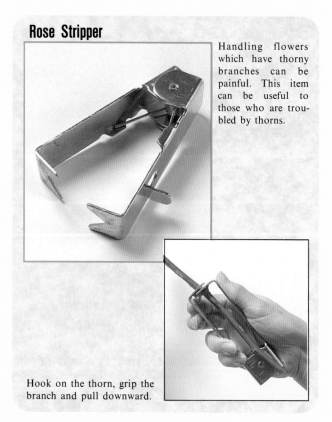

Hook on the thorn, grip the branch and pull downward.

Cutting with a Florist Knife

Hold the knife facing yourself and pull ball back to cut.

To make the largest surface possible for water absorption, cut on a diagonal angle.

Cutting with Flower Scissors

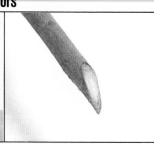

Position scissors at an angle to the branch and cut in one motion.

Branches should be cut on an angle if possible.

Vases and Accessories

Variety of Vases

One of the charms of flower arranging is choosing the vase. Vases come in a variety of materials including pottery, porcelain and glass. There's no end to the kinds of size, shape, color and pattern available. Look for a vase which is pleasing to you and easy to use. By using oasis the choices are unlimited.

By using cute accessories well, your arrangement comes alive in unexpected ways. Buy at the florist's, stuffed toy store or toy shop as found to have on supply. The variety of arrangements broadens and becomes doubly enjoyable.

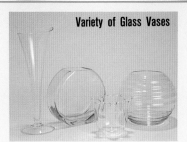

Variety of Glass Vases

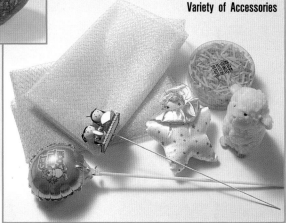

Variety of Accessories

Accessories for use with Bouquets, Corsages, etc.

Wiring and taping are used. The larger the number the thinner the wire. Wire comes in white, green and other colors. Floral tape comes in a variety of colors, as well.
When finished arranging, be sure to mist the flowers. A corsage in a corsage box is a charming and useful way to give a present.

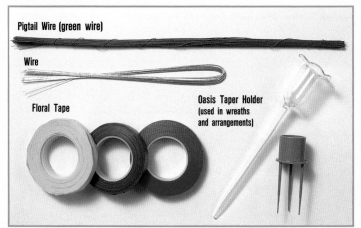

Pigtail Wire (green wire)

Wire

Floral Tape

Oasis Taper Holder
(used in wreaths
and arrangements)

Sprayer

Corsage Box

Conditioning

Flowers are living things needing to be handled with care to prolong their lifespan. From the grower's to the marketplace, from marketplace to the florist, time passes. Though the florist waters them to keep them fresh, place the flowers in water soon after buying them.

For most flowers, cutting the stem on an angle 1~1½″ (3~4 cm) above the bottom and placing in water is enough. Cutting on an angle is done to make a larger area from which to absorb water. Cut as cleanly as possible to avoid damaging the veins. (Refer to scissors on page 48) Depending on the material, steps such as soaking in hot water and watering upside down are necessary. 70~80% in bloom is said to be the most beautiful in arrangements. Keep a careful eye on the flowers, as if much time passes before assembling the arrangement the flowers may open.

Hot Water Treatment for Chrysanthemums and Long Stemmed Roses

Hot water treatment is effective.
1 Boil water in an old pan. With ends together wrap the flowers in a newspaper and secure at the bottom. Put the stems in the boiling water for 30 seconds to 1 minute.
2 Remove immediately to cold water to soak.

Soaking Snowball

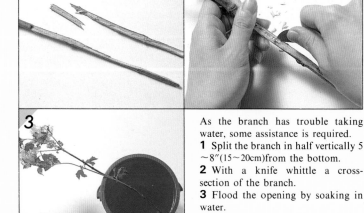

As the branch has trouble taking water, some assistance is required.
1 Split the branch in half vertically 5~8″(15~20cm)from the bottom.
2 With a knife whittle a cross-section of the branch.
3 Flood the opening by soaking in water.

For Long Lasting Flowers

To keep flowers for a long time after arranging, water maintainance is essential. Be sure to change the water every day if possible.

Misting with a sprayer can protect from dehydration and encourage longevity.

Measuring Using the Body

Using a ruler or measuring tape to measure each step is time-consuming. Familiarizing yourself with the length of parts of your body is very handy. Oddly enough, arrangements measured by hands are sized correctly to the maker and have a relaxed sense. Bouquets and corsages are especially so. Measure needed parts now for future reference. They will be useful in other areas of life as well.

One Hand's Length

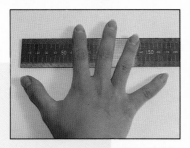

Measured from the tip of the thumb to the tip of the little finger, it is the fundamental body measure. Between 7~8″(17~20cm.).

Two Hands' Length

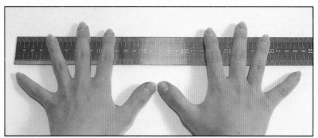

Two hands' length is simply double a single hand's length. In general a woman's double hand length is approximately 13~16″ (34~40cm.).
Once a single hand's length is known, it is possible to measure any multiple.

Wrist to Elbow Length

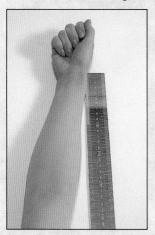

The length from wrist to elbow is said to be the same as the length of the foot. Measure to check. This is a useful measurement to remeber.

Arrangement Size

Before beginning to arrange, estimate the approximate size. This book has used a 2 hands' length as its largest size. Depending on the place for display, the purpose and the vase adjust to achieve good balance.

Measuring Flowers

Turn the flower upside down touching the vase to measure. Always remember to add enough extra to insert in oasis.

Colorful Arrangements

Using a haphazard variety of colors yields an arrangement without unifying structure. Choosing flowers is the opportunity to manipulate colors and show your personal sense. Be careful not to spoil the flower's sweetness and give full expression to each flower as it is placed.

Flower Hues 1

In order to understand varied colored arrangements, a color graph was constructed as a standard for arrangements. Use it as a guide for arranging. Insert pale flowers first gradually progressing toward the darker shades.

Floral Materials Delphinium, Rose, Star-of-Bethlehem, Nerine, Marguerite, Tulip, African Daisy, Alstroemeria, Sweet Pea, Oncidium, Triplet Lily, Perezii, Scabiosa, Lilac, Stock, Cyclamen, Sandersonia, Carnation, Asparagus Fern, Smilax Asparagus, Bear Grass

Anemone Arrangement

Pastel Color Flower Basket

Choosing an all pastel tone is one possibility. Adding baby's breath to pale pink and blue flowers yields a soft finish.

Floral Materials Tulip, Spray Carnation, Blue Star, Baby's Breath, Leather Fern, Eucalyptus, Wheat Stalks

Using different colors of the same floral materials is an easy method. Each was arranged considering its individual form.

Floral Materials Anemone, Wheat Stalks, Eucalyptus, Diamond Ivy

Flower Hues 2

Even when strongly individual floral materials seem disparate, use of greens and baby's breath can pull it all together gorgeously. Take care that each flower is showing best.

Floral Materials Snapdragon, African Daisy, Lily, Rose, Iris, Statice, Fresia, Marguerite, Baby's Breath, Bear Grass

Candle Arrangements

Beautiful candles are available. They are lovely for Christmas, but why not include them in every day arrangements ? They are a beautiful accent for flowers.

Falling Star Flower Box
(Bright Yellow Candle)

A starry sky image arranged in a round present box. If it appears that a fairy tale is springing from the box, it is a big success.

Floral Materials Magnolia Praecocissima, Marguerite, Baby's Breath, Tulip, Spray Carnation, Mimosa Acacia, Eryngium, Asparagus Fern

White Candle

Floral Materials Rose(Tineke), Carnation, Calla Lily, Spray Mum, Stock, Bishop's Weed, Wheat Stalks, Dracaena, Asparagus Fern, Diamond Ivy, Bear Grass

Light Green Candle

Floral Materials Rose(Sonia), African Daisy, Wheat Stalks, Asparagus Macowanii, Diamond Ivy

Pink Almond Candle

Floral Materials Rose(Bridal Pink), Perezii, Asparagus Macowanii, Wheat Stalks, Ladder Fern

Ruby Candle

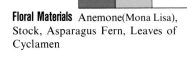

Floral Materials Anemone(Mona Lisa), Stock, Asparagus Fern, Leaves of Cyclamen

Heartfelt Floral Presents

Concerts, birthdays, dance recitals and parties are amongst the many chances to give the gift of flowers. By pairing a unique idea with personal sense a new kind of present emerges.

Concerts

A gorgeous bouquet arranged for a bright day. Use of *washi* paper and an elaborate bow makes the wrapping lavish.

Floral Materials Delphinium, Marguerite, Iris, Viburnum, Magnolia Praecocissima, Baby's Breath, Misty Blue, Celastrus Orbiculatus, Bear Grass

For Father's Day

How about this arrangement to show your everlasting, wholehearted appreciation ? Given with a bottle of his favorite wine, you are sure to see his face light up.

Floral Materials Rose(Tineke), Glory Lily, Asparagus Fern, Bear Grass

Christmas Season Hostess Gift

This is a reverse **L** shaped arrangement. (see page 22) Ready to be displayed and not overwieldy, this flower basket is a thoughtful gift for your host or hostess.

Floral Materials Carnation, Spray Mum, Bouvardia, Alchemilla Berries, Leather Fern

Wrap in cellophane and attach a bow with a staple to create an easy way to carry this arrangement. The miniature dolls are effective in tying the theme together. Buying these accessories when you see them to have on hand is very convenient.

Floral Materials Higan-zakura(cherry), Field Mustard, Tulip

For Get Well Visits

For those confined to bed it's best to choose bright flowers with little scent. Use favorite flowers, if known, as the central point and add fruit.

Floral Materials Delphinium, Rose(Sonia), Spray Mum

For Mother's Day

Hiding perfume or a handkerchief in the basket is a fresh idea. Mom will be happy to receive her favorite flowers.

Floral Materials Carnation, Dendrobium Phalaenopsis(Bridal White), Leather Fern, Eucalyptus

Valentine's Day

Entrust your heart to this poodle. Carnations are gathered together to make head and body. Front legs and tail are formed by one bud each. Use buttons for eyes and nose, filling extra space with accenting flowers.

Cut short stems and insert flowers into a heart shaped oasis. Make with a variety of different flowers.

Floral Materials Carnations
Outside edge : A variety including Sweet Pea

Floral Materials
Spray Carnations, Roses

59

For a small hostess gift or
for sale at bazaars.

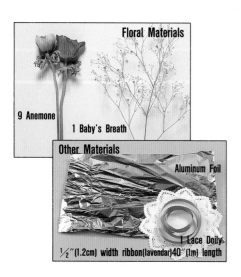

Floral Materials

1 Asparagus Fern

3 Spray
Carnations

2 Blue Star

Other: Baby's Breath

Hand-sized basket

Mini Basket

Place cellophane and then
oasis in basket. Insert asparagus fern at random.

Cut spray carnations to a
short length and insert for
good balance at a variety of
heights.

Separate baby's breath into
short pieces and insert so as
not to come out to the level
of the flowers.

Add blue star. Cut into sev-
eral pieces and insert in
between carnations to finish.

Anemone Bouquet

A perfect present for events such as birth-
day paries. Baby's breath gives a soft finish. It is easy to make and can be done
with a variety of flowers.

Floral Materials

9 Anemone

1 Baby's Breath

Other Materials

Aluminum Foil

1 Lace Doily

½″(1.2cm) width ribbon(lavendar)40″(1m) length

Cut to the center and make a
number of incisions from the
central point.

Slightly overlap the edge and
secure with cellophane tape.

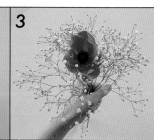

Surround central anemone
with baby's breath.

With stems even wrap 2~3
times with a rubber band
and secure.

Insert base through prepared
doily.

Place stems on aluminum
foil which has had the ends
folded over.

Flower baskets are welcome gifts as they can be displayed immediately. They are easy for the beginner to achieve.

Floral Materials

1 Eucalyptus

3 Spray Mum (Pinky)

1 Leather Fern

Set cellophane in the basket and secure Oasis.

Spray Mum Basket

1 Insert leather fern in the front side section of oasis in a dangling shape.

2 Bend each spray mum individually back from the branch, cut on an angle and insert in oasis.

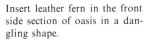

3 Separate the leftover leather fern and insert randomly in back of flowers.

4 Side view. Add Eucalyptus in empty spaces to finish.

4 Add remaining anemone, baby's breath to make a round figure.

5 Grasp firmly and cut evenly leaving 1~1½"(3~4cm).

9 Fold aluminum foil in half encasing the stems and wrap.

10 Wrap a ribbon aronud the base and tie in a bow.

Enjoying Seasonal Arrangements

Wouldn't it be wonderful to always feel the seasons inside our homes ? Between seasons, especially, try to keep heartfelt arrangements of flowers.

New Year's Arrangement

Using pine as the base, the happy colors red and white were used for the New Year. Bright red *washi* paper, the color of the first sunrise, wraps the arrangement and it is tied with gold and silver cords.

Floral Materials Pine, Japanese Quince, Camelia, Miniature Chrysanthemums, Dendrobium Phalaenopsis, Cymbidium, Lily, Rose, Nandina, Asparagus Macowanii, Viscum Album

Beautifully arranged in a container made from bamboo. Even without a proper display corner, this arrangement fills the room with spring. Elegant Lilies were chosen to be symbolic of the future and inserted as buds.

Floral Materials Pine, Candlestick Lily, Prianthus Narcissus, Daffodil, Asparagus Macowanii

Arrange colorful flowers of spring to celebrate the girl's festival. This is a happy day for both children and adults alike.

Floral Materials Higan-zakura(cherry), Tulip, Field Mustard, Viscum Album

Children's Day Arrangement

All parents around the world pray for the health and happiness of their children. Arranged with a robust, refreshing sense.

Floral Materials Iris, Calla Lily, Gold-Dust Dracaenas, Bear Grass

Triangular Shaped Style

Arrangement for a Summer Day

For an image of southern islands passionate, red flowers were arranged in a coconut vase. Using shells is also nice for summer arrangements.

Floral Materials Anthurium, Glory Lily, Perezii, Bishop's weed, Bear Grass, Window Plant

Summer Lei

Flowers floating in a glass dish cool down a summer day. Use well soaked flowers to enjoy creating leis. Share with chidren to forget the summer heat.

Floral Materials
7 Dendrobium Phalaenopsis,
3 Spray Carnations

Instructions:
Thread a long needle with strong cotton thread. Alternate 5 dendrobium and 1 carnation repeating until long enough to put over head. Tie ends together to finish.

Moon Viewing Arrangement

This arrangement for moon viewing makes the most of the beautiful line of bear grass. Just the thing for a quiet, autumn night.

Floral Materials Fennel, Aster, Erynguim, Blue Fantasia, Bear Grass, Callistemon

Christmas Wreath (Instructions page 66)

The wreath's circular shape is symbolic of endless faith and the eternal love and everlasting life of Christ. This symbol made from greens is to hang on the door at Christmas. Try making one from live materials this year.

Christmas Wreath

Use whatever red berries are available. Cut 2 #20 wires in half to wire the pine cones. Divide the remainder equally into 6 parts each and bend in a **U** shape. Make about 100. (Refer to photo below)

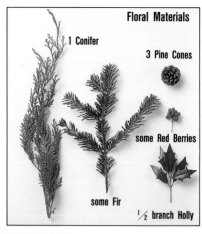

Floral Materials

1 Conifer

3 Pine Cones

some Red Berries

some Fir

1/2 branch Holly

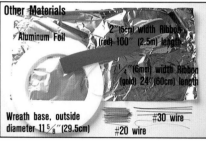

Other Materials

Aluminum Foil

2″ (5cm) width Ribbon (red) 100″ (2.5m) length

1/4″ (6mm) width Ribbon (gold) 24″ (60cm) length

Wreath base, outside diameter 11 5/8″ (29.5cm)

#30 wire

#20 wire

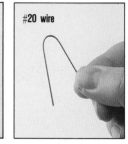

#20 wire

Pine Cones

1

Cut a #20 wire in half and hook over the bottom of the pine cone.

2

Wrap the long side of the wire over the short 2~3 times.

3

Bend the wire back to make an **L** shape easy to insert, and set aside.

Ribbon

Make ribbon as per page 44 without tying in the middle. Use a #30 wire to secure.

Wreath Base

1

The back side of the aluminum foil faces out. Divide the foil in 3 equal lengths and cut.

2

To cover wreath start from the back of the base. When one piece runs out, overlap with next about 3/4″ (2cm) to continue.

3

Cover form completely. The front side of the base may remain uncovered white.

4

Insert one of the **U** pins into the places where the foil overlaps.

2

Attach conifer. Place following the curve of the base. Overlap in the same direction.

3

Secure with **U** wires point by point. Cover the whole base.

4

Completely cover the side of the base, taking care not to leave any spaces.

5

Do the same with the inside curve. Firmly secure with **U** wires to ensure nothing falls.

6

After completely covering with conifer the whole should be completely covered leaving no white spaces.

7

Insert 4~5 holly facing towards the top. Do not place where the ribbon will be.

8

Insert short pieces of fir. Position facing upwards over all but the area where the ribbon will be. Insert on sides as well.

9

Insert red berries. Facing upwards distribute over whole except for the location of the ribbon and secure weth **U** wires. Insert on sides as well.

10

Place the 3 pine cones for accent securing by inserting wire into frame.

11

Secure the red bow in the middle with wire. Fasten gold ribbon securely for hanging.

Arrangements from Gift Flowers

Not only have the opportunities to give flowers increased, but so have the chances to be on the receiving end. It would be shame not to make the most of them and make a beautiful arrangement. By knowing the basics, received flowers can be turned into expert arrangements.

From a Spring Bouquet

For Living Room
Floral Materials Mimosa Acacia, Calla Lily, Oncidium, Bear Grass, Alexandrian Laurel

For Children's Room
Floral Materials Tulip, Mimosa Acacia, Oncidium, Alexandrian Laurel

A bouquet of everyday spring flowers was received. The flowers were skillfully divided into those for the living room and some for a child's room, then arranged each in its own basket. Stuffed animals were added to the child's basket for a touch of fun. They bring spring to the room.

From a Tulip Bouquet

The variety of tulips is growing, with many sweet tulips becoming available. A bouquet of soft lilac, misty blue and tulips was received. Arrange roughly in a clear, glass container. It is a free and elegant arrangement.

Floral Materials Tulip, Lilac, Misty Blue, Asparagus Fern

From a Red Bouquet (see page right)

These are strong flowers with a strong presence. Thinking of overall balance, a black vase was chosen as the two complement each other. They were arranged to bring out a slight softness amidst the relaxed, natural feeling which suggests the movement of wind.

Floral Materials Anthurium, Glory Lily, Asparagus Fern

Containers from Everyday Items

Place oasis in a soda can, cover with 2 paper napkins overlapped and tie with a bow for a lovely touch. A nice present to please a good friend.

(Directions page 74)

From table settings to kitchen tools, flower containers can be made from things at hand. From the obvious sugar bowl, pitcher, wine cooler and bucket, to the not so obvious aluminum cans, soda bottles and even ladles, wonderful arrangements can emerge. The important factor is to arrange the materials beautifully. Fully exploit the possibilites of the idea and personal sense.

Kitchen Ladle Arrangement

Oasis is securely positioned with oasis tape. For a kitchen accent use herbs and spices and enjoy using them straight from the arrangement.

72

Kitchen Goods to use as Containers

Aluminum Can

Soup Tureen

Table Basket

Milk Pitcher

Ladle

Sugar Bowl

Various Pitchers

Take a fresh look around the kitchen. You need not own a magnificent vase to make a beautiful arrangement, as there are lots of possibilities in your kitchen. Enjoy freely arrangements using the potential of each item.

Ladle Arrangement

Floral Materials 1 Anemone(red), 1 Anemone(white), 1 Stock, 3 Bishop's Weeds, 1 Statice, some Asparagus Fern, Asparagus, Diamond Ivy
Other Materials Ribbon

Cut oasis slightly smaller than the ladle, soak well and secure with oasis tape.

Wrap ribbon carefully around the handle taking care not to leave any gaps. Tie the ends to secure.

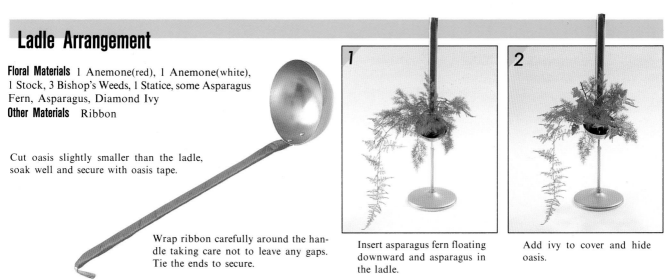

1 Insert asparagus fern floating downward and asparagus in the ladle.

2 Add ivy to cover and hide oasis.

3 Add red anemone which has been cut short in the middle for the focal point.

4 Add 2 statice on either side under anemone so as not to reach as far as the flower.

5 Add stock which has been cut short and the white anemone around the red one.

6 Add bishop's weed rounding off to finish.

Aluminum Can Arrangement

Flowers left over from making a larger arrangement were placed in an aluminum can. Choose beautiful paper napkins which coordinate with the flowers and none will know. Cut oasis to the size of the can and soak well. Plastic containers can also be used.

Place one napkin at an angle on the other, wrap the can and secure with a rubber band. Use the 2 ribbons to cover and tie a bow.

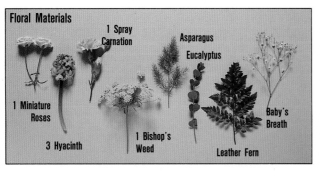

Floral Materials

1 Miniature Roses
3 Hyacinth
1 Spray Carnation
1 Bishop's Weed
Asparagus
Eucalyptus
Leather Fern
Baby's Breath

1 Cut a miniature rose to a length slightly longer than the can. Insert upright in the center.

2 Cut 2 more the same length. Insert **1** on either side horizontally or sloping down.

3 Cut the 3 hyacinths to different lengths slightly shorter than the rose. Insert at various angles.

4 Add roses and carnations between **1** and **2** so as not to protrude past original flowers. Add roses horizontally in the front.

5 Use remaining roses and carnations to fill in the gaps. Place so as not to come out as far as previous flowers. Cover the whole.

6 Add the rest of the flowers and greens for good balance. Add 3 leather ferns in front and one in back to tie it all together.

Flower Preservation

Dried Flowers and Potpourri Arrangements

The desire to keep flowers with special memories and retain beauty can turn to reality by drying flowers and making potpourri.

Flowers which have kept a beautiful shape can be arranged with the stems attached. This wreath was made using a store bought wreath base and sahara (the dry version of oasis) keeping the image of a field for inspiration.

Potpourri

When only the petals are left, potpourri can be made to enjoy lasting fragrance.

Top right — Placed in a beautiful dish it becomes a room accent.

Top left — Lace sewn into a small bag was filled with potpourri and tied with a ribbon to form a sachet.

Handmade Potpourri Decoration(directions page 77)

Dried Flowers

Natural Drying

Make light bundles of flowers and hang upside down. If air circulation is good, flowers will dry in a week to 10 days depending on the flowers. Baby's breath, statice, mimosa acacia and asters are among the good choices for drying. Roses can be beautifully dried, but some varieties loose their color.

Potpourri

Combining pleasant fragrances to create your own fragrance is the fun of potpourri. Collect flowers and leaves and dry well to make. When there is little fragrance, add essence oils to add perfume. From house to car, pocket to handbag, there are many ways to enjoy potpourri.

Silicone Preservation

Silicone gel preserves flowers by artificial dehydration. Flowers retain their color and shape. Use silicone gel sold packaged for drying flowers. Any sort of container can be used, but one with some height allows enough space to fit the flower. The gel is not poisonous, but it is better to use a container not used for food preparation.

1 Place cut flower on top of $\frac{3}{4} \sim 1''(2 \sim 3\text{cm})$ of silicone gel.
2 Cover flower completely with silicone gel so that it cannot be seen.
3 Close lid and mark date.
4 It dries in $5 \sim 7$ days. Gently pour out the gel and retrieve flower.

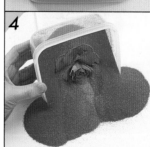

Gather as many dried flowers and leaves as possible choosing those with pleasant fragrances and colors.

Mix ingredients and add desired flower essence.

Mix well. Some materials give off more fragrance when broken or crushed.

Store in a sealed container for $2 \sim 3$ days. When desired fragrance is achieved used as desired.